Our Passover Lamb
A Christian Haggadah

Freedom Hill Community

PO Box 1865, Saint Charles, MO 63302-1865 USA

www.freedomhillcommuntiy.com

Comments and questions: www.freedomhillcommunity.com

Our Passover Lamb
A Christian Haggadah

This day shall be for you a memorial day, and you shall keep it as a feast to the Lord; throughout your generations, as a statute forever, you shall keep it as a feast.

-Exodus 12:14

Cleanse out the old leaven that you may be a new lump, as you really are unleavened. For Christ, our Passover lamb, has been sacrificed. Let us therefore celebrate the festival, not with the old leaven, the leaven of malice and evil, but with the unleavened bread of sincerity and truth.

-1 Corinthians 5:7-8

What You'll Need

1. Matzah crackers
2. Parsley
3. Salt water
4. Horseradish
5. Charoseth—mixture of apples, nuts, honey
6. Lamb shank bone
7. Wine/grape juice
8. Two large candles
9. Bowl (for hand washing)
10. Water pitcher (for hand washing)
11. Decorated cup (Elijah's cup)
12. Cloth (afikomen cover)
13. Plates and glasses for each guest

Passover

Let the people of Israel keep the Passover at its appointed time.

Numbers 9:2

One of the most important annual events on the Hebrew calendar is the Passover meal and the seven-day Feast of Unleavened Bread. This powerful biblical holiday commemorates the Exodus story—the deliverance of Israel from their slavery in ancient Egypt.

The story of Passover is recorded in the book of Exodus. It takes place in Egypt, where the people of Israel were slaves. One day the Israelites cried out to God for deliverance, so God sent Moses to go to the ruler of Egypt, Pharaoh, and order him to let the Israelites go free. Pharaoh refused, so God sent plagues upon the land of Egypt: frogs, locusts, and boils, among others (Exodus 7-10). But even after suffering these plagues, Pharaoh still refused to let the Israelites go.

Since Pharaoh continued to stubbornly resist God's will, God told Moses that He was going to send one last plague upon the land—the death of the firstborn son in every home in Egypt. However, God provided a means of safety for the Israelites. He told Moses that He would not touch the houses that had the blood of a lamb on their doorposts. So Moses told the Israelites to kill a lamb and spread its blood on the doorposts of their houses, and thus those houses were "passed over" by God and spared from the plague.

After suffering through this terrible plague, Pharaoh finally agreed to let the Israelites go free, and all of God's people quickly followed Moses out of Egypt. However, after a short while, Pharaoh ordered his army to go after them, and they chased the Israelites to the bank of the Red Sea. God split the sea, creating a path for the Israelites to cross. But after they crossed, the Egyptian army continued to chase them. So God caused the sea to crash down on the Egyptians, covering them in the water.

Thus, the Israelites were delivered from Egypt and began their journey to the Promised Land. And the Feast of Passover was established to commemorate this miraculous story.

How is Passover Relevant to Christians?

The simplest answer to this question is that God commanded His people to keep Passover and Unleavened Bread throughout their generations as a statute forever (Exodus 12:14). Thus, if you consider yourself a follower of the God of Israel, this is something you are to do forever.

Also, during the last supper before His crucifixion, Yeshua told His disciples to "do *this* in remembrance of me" (Luke 22:19, emphasis added). What were they doing when Yeshua said that to His disciples? If we look a few verses earlier, we see that they were doing a Passover seder. Indeed, if you are a follower of the Messiah, you are to do Passover in remembrance of Yeshua.

Not only is Passover commanded by God and reiterated by Yeshua, but even the apostle Paul tells Christians to observe this feast:

> Cleanse out the old leaven that you may be a new lump, as you really are unleavened. For Christ, our Passover lamb, has been sacrificed. **Let us therefore celebrate the festival**, not with the old leaven, the leaven of malice and evil, but with the unleavened bread of sincerity and truth. (1 Corinthians 5:7-8, emphasis added)

So the simple answer is that God repeatedly told us to observe Passover and then reiterated that command through Messiah and the apostle Paul. Therefore, Passover is relevant to Christians. But it goes much deeper than that. The story of Israel's deliverance from Egypt is a prophetic picture of our own deliverance from our slavery to sin. It's all about the Gospel. Thus, the story of Passover is our story too. And God wants us to always remember this story. He wants us to always reflect on His love for us and that He gave His Only Son so that we can be free.

3

Removing the Leaven

During the days leading up to Passover, we are to remove all of the leaven (*chametz*) from our homes (Exodus 12:15). Leaven is a substance that is added to dough to cause it to ferment and rise. In the Bible, leaven is often symbolic of sin. Thus, the command to remove leaven from our homes is designed to teach us to examine our hearts. It is a time of introspection. As we explore every corner of every room in our homes for literal leaven, we are to ask God to search every corner of our hearts to reveal any sin in our lives.

Bedikat Chametz (The Search for Leaven)

On the day before Passover, it is customary to do a final search around the house for leaven. This is called *bedikat chametz*, which means "search for leaven." For fun, parents usually hide a few pieces of leavened bread around the house so that their children will have something to find. It is customary to turn off all the lights in the house and use a candle or flashlight during the search. The candle or flashlight represents Yeshua, who is "the light of the world" (John 8:12). It's by His light that we can overcome sin in our lives. A blessing can be said before beginning the search:

HEBREW:

*Baruch attah Adonai Eloheinu melech ha-olam asher
kidishanu, bemitzvotav vetzivanu al bi'ur chametz*

ENGLISH:

Blessed are you, Lord our God, King of the universe, who
has sanctified us with his commandments, and commanded
us concerning the removal of chametz.

After leaven is found, the children are to call for their father to
come and sweep it up. This teaches us that we are unable to remove sin
from our lives on our own. We need our Father in heaven's help. Once
all the leaven is found, it is gathered together to be burned or thrown
away. This symbolizes how Yeshua frees us from sin and removes it
from our lives.

As far as the east is from the west, so far has He removed our
transgressions from us. (Psalm 103:12)

If we confess our sins, he is faithful and just to forgive us our
sins and to cleanse us from all unrighteousness. (1 John 1:9)

Suggestions

- This Haggadah serves as a basic step-by-step guide to the Seder. Feel free to go into more depth as you speak on the meanings behind each tradition.

- Invite friends and neighbors over to your Seder.

- Try to get everyone to participate.

- Allow different members of your family to read different parts.

- If you don't know the Hebrew blessings, write them out on a piece of paper so that the members of your Seder can read along with you when you pray them.

Welcome to the Seder!

SEDER LEADER:

Tonight is the night that we celebrate the Passover. We celebrate to remember how God freed His people from the hand of the Egyptians, but also how the real Lamb of God, Yeshua, freed us from sin. The telling of this story is called the *Haggadah*, which means, "the telling," and the ceremony itself is called a *Seder* which means, "order." During this Seder, we will be partaking in special foods that help us reconnect with the journey of the Israelites coming out of Egypt, and also recall our own spiritual journey of coming out of sin.

Even though the story of the original Passover is central to the season of Passover, for believers in Yeshua, we will see the story of Messiah as the Lamb of God, and the story of our own lives, woven into each part of the Passover Seder.

READER:

"And you shall observe this event as an ordinance for you and your children forever. When you enter the land which the Lord will give you, as He has promised, you shall observe this rite. And when your children say to you, 'What does this rite mean to you?' you shall say, 'It is a Passover sacrifice to the Lord who passed over the houses of the sons of Israel in Egypt when He smote the Egyptians, but spared our homes." (Exodus 12:24-27)

READER:

"And he took bread, and when he had given thanks, he broke it and gave it to them, saying, 'This is my body, which is given for you. Do this in remembrance of me.' And likewise the cup after they had eaten, saying, 'This cup that is poured out for you is the new covenant in my blood.'" (Luke 22:19-20)

READER:

"Clean out the old leaven so that you may be a new lump, just as you are in fact unleavened. For Christ our Passover also has been sacrificed. Therefore let us celebrate the feast, not with old leaven, nor with the leaven of malice and wickedness, but with the unleavened bread of sincerity and truth." (1 Corinthians 5:7-8)

The Seder Plate

SEDER LEADER:

In front of you this evening is the traditional Seder plate that contains all of the items we will be using to tell the story of Passover. Each of these items is symbolic of the Israelites' journey out of Egypt. Since in Scripture the Exodus from Egypt serves as a model of redemption for all time, there is an additional layer of depth as we look at how each part of the Israelites' story relates to our own journey out of slavery to sin.

[Seder Leader explains each part of the Seder plate.]

Karpas – Parsley. This represents the growth of the Israelites and God's blessing on them as promised to Abraham.

Maror – A bitter herb, such as horseradish. This represents the bitterness of slavery and reminds us of the bitterness that comes as a result of our sins.

Charoseth – A mixture of apples, nuts, and honey. This represents the mortar that the slaves in Egypt used to make bricks. It also reminds us of the sweetness of God's grace.

Matzah – Flat, unleavened bread. This represents the bread made by the Israelites when they left Egypt. They didn't have time for their bread to rise because they left "in haste" (Deuteronomy 16:3). This is to help us recall our deliverance from Egypt and remind us that we need to get the leaven (sin) out of our lives.

Ze'roa – A roasted lamb shank bone. This represents the Passover sacrifice whose blood was spread over the doorposts of the Israelite homes in Egypt. It also represents the Messiah Yeshua, the lamb of God who takes away the sin of the world.

Wine/Grape Juice – The wine is representative of the blood of Yeshua that was shed for us (Matthew 26:27-28).

The Four Cups of Wine

SEDER LEADER:

During our Seder, there are four cups of wine. These cups stand for the four "I will" statements found in Exodus.

READER:

"Say therefore to the people of Israel, 'I am the Lord, and I will bring you out from under the burdens of the Egyptians, and I will deliver you from slavery to them, and I will redeem you with an outstretched arm and with great acts of judgment. I will take you to be my people, and I will be your God, and you shall know that I am the Lord your God, who has brought you out from under the burdens of the Egyptians." (Exodus 6:6-7)

[Seder Leader explains the four cups of wine.]

1) The Cup of Sanctification — "I will bring you out."

2) The Cup of Deliverance — "I will deliver you."

3) The Cup of Redemption — "I will redeem you."

4) The Cup of Praise — "I will take you to be my people."

Lighting of the Candles

SEDER LEADER:

Before we begin our Seder, we will light the two candles before us. The light from the candles reminds us that we are commanded to let our light shine before men so that they might see our good works and glorify our Father in heaven. Light dispels the darkness. We as Yeshua's disciples must dispel the darkness of this world by living according to His commandments, loving God, and loving our neighbor.

Traditionally, the female head of the household will light the candles and close her eyes while waving her hands from the candles toward her eyes. This symbolizes inviting the Light of the World, Yeshua, to come into our lives.

[Woman lights the candles.]

[Woman says the following prayer.]

HEBREW:

Baruch atah adonai eloheinu melech ha'olam, asher kideshanoo, be'mitzvotav vetzivanoo lehiyot or lagoyim v'natan lanu et Yeshua Mechicheinu or haolam.

ENGLISH:

Blessed are you, Lord our God, King of the universe, who sanctifies us with your commandments, and has commanded us to be a light to the nations, and gave to us Yeshua, our Messiah, the light of the world.

Washing of Our Hands

SEDER LEADER:

Before we begin, we will wash our hands, representing the washing of the water of the Word. In order to go into the Temple of God in ancient Israel, the priest had to first wash himself in the water of the Brazen Laver. In the same way, no one comes to the Father except through the Son, who cleanses us from sin. On the night of the Last Supper, Yeshua showed His true servant nature by washing the feet of His disciples. In the same way, let us each help wash the hands to the person to our left.

[Each person pours a small amount of water over the person's hands to their left over a bowl.]

The First Cup of Wine

The Cup of Sanctification

[Seder Leader holds up the first up and says *Kadosh*, which means, "Holy."]

SEADER LEADER:

This cup represents the first "I will" from Exodus 6:6-7. The Lord promises to bring us out from under the burdens of Egypt and sanctify us. Drinking this cup is a declaration of our choice to be holy—*kadosh*—from the world by following God's ways.

READER:

Yeshua sanctifies His followers and sets them apart from the rest of the world: "Before him will be gathered all the nations, and he will separate people one from another as a shepherd separates the sheep from the goats." (Matthew 25:32)

[Seder Leader asks everyone to hold up their glass of wine. In his own words, he then thanks God for choosing us to be holy in His Name.]

[Everyone recites the blessing over the wine.]

HEBREW:

Baruch atah Adonai Eloheinu melech ha-olam borei p'ri hagafen.

ENGLISH:

Blessed are you, Lord our God, King of the universe, who creates the fruit of the vine.

[Everyone drinks the first cup.]

Karpas

Eating of the Parsley

SEDER LEADER:

The parsley represents the growth of the Israelites and God's blessing on them as promised to Abraham. It also reminds us of the tears that were shed in Egypt by the children of God because of their harsh slavery.

In addition, it reminds us of the pain and sorrow that come as a result of our sin. Before we met Yeshua the Messiah, we were separated from God and therefore couldn't know true joy. Praise God for the new life we have in Yeshua!

[Everyone recites the blessing over the parsley.]

HEBREW:

Baruch atah Adonai Eloheinu melech ha-olam borei p'ri ha-adama.

ENGLISH:

Blessed are you, Lord our God, King of the universe, who creates the fruit of the earth.

LEADER:

Dip the parsley in the salt water twice and shake the salt water from the parsley to symbolize the tears of our forefathers.

[Everyone takes some parsley, dips it into the salt water twice, and then eats it.]

Yachatz

Breaking the Matzah

SEDER LEADER:

The matzah (unleavened bread) is kept in a special covering with three compartments representing the triune nature of God—Father, Son, and Holy Spirit. One piece of matzah is placed in each compartment. In Judaism, the three pieces of matzah are said to represent Abraham, Isaac, and Jacob. The middle matzah represents Isaac, the son of Abraham, who willingly submitted to his father to be a sacrifice (Genesis 22). This is a beautiful picture of Yeshua, the Son of God, who willingly laid down His life for us.

READER:

But he was pierced for our transgressions; he was crushed for our iniquities; upon him was the chastisement that brought us peace, and with his wounds we are healed. All we like sheep have gone astray; we have turned—every one—to his own way; and the Lord has laid on him the iniquity of us all. (Isaiah 53:5-6)

SEDER LEADER:

Just as Yeshua was broken for our transgressions, so we take the middle piece of matzah and break it in two. One half of the broken matzah is placed back into the covering while the other half is wrapped in a separate linen cloth. This piece is called the *afikomen*, which means, "that which comes after," or "dessert." The afikomen is then hidden until after the seder. This represents Yeshua's body on earth. After He was crucified, his body was wrapped in cloth, and then He was hidden away in the tomb.

READER:

And Joseph took the body and wrapped it in a clean linen shroud and laid it in his own new tomb, which he had cut in the rock. And he rolled a great stone to the entrance of the tomb and went away. (Matthew 27:59-60)

[Seder Leader breaks the middle matzah, wraps the larger piece of matzah in a piece of white linen or cloth, and hides the afikomen.]

The Four Questions

[Four people at the seder (preferably the youngest children) ask the four questions.]

READER:

On all other nights we eat either leavened or unleavened bread. Why on this night do we eat only matzah, the unleavened bread?

SEDER LEADER:

We eat matzah to remember that the Israelites left Egypt in haste. There was no time to wait for the bread to rise. Therefore, the purpose of eating unleavened bread is to help us recall our deliverance from Egypt. God wants us to remember that the basis for our relationship with Him is that He delivers us (Exodus 6:2-8). There is nothing we have done to earn His love. He "heard the groaning of His people" and acted simply on the basis of His great love. For believers in Messiah Yeshua, eating matzah has an additional layer of depth. Yeshua, our Passover lamb, has delivered us from the slavery of our sin—our own "Egypt." Therefore, eating matzah is also a reminder of the Gospel through Yeshua.

READER:

On all other nights we eat all kinds of foods. Why on this night do we eat only bitter herbs?

SEDER LEADER:

We eat bitter herbs to remember the bitterness of our bondage to sin. Just as the Israelites were in slavery to the Egyptians, we were in slavery to our sins until Yeshua delivered us.

READER:

On all other nights we do not dip herbs even once into salt water. Why on this night do we dip twice?

SEDER LEADER:

We dip the parsley in salt water to remember the tears of the Israelites in Egyptian slavery and also our tears that come as a result of our sins.

READER:

On all other nights we eat either sitting upright or reclining. Why on this night do we eat reclining?

SEDER LEADER:

On this night we show our freedom by reclining. In ancient Egypt, only free men could do this. Since we are free from the slavery of sin, we can now "recline" with the Lord.

SEDER LEADER:

At this time, please pour your second cup of wine. It is poured at the beginning of the telling of the story of the Exodus to remind us that even through all the plagues and trials of life, His redemption is always near. It is found in the blood of His Son, Yeshua.

The Story of Passover

The story of Israel's deliverance from Egypt is to be retold to our children at the time of Passover every year (see Exodus 12:24-28 & 13:8-9). We can learn many lessons from the Exodus story and what it means to us as Christians today. The Exodus teaches us about standing on God's promises in the face of extreme opposition. It teaches us that, in the midst of the plagues and trials of life, God is with His people. Most importantly, it teaches us about our own salvation in Yeshua.

The command to remember and retell this story can be fulfilled in many ways. If you have kids at your Seder table, the following pages contain a simple telling of the story that they would enjoy.

Passover Story for Kids

There once was an evil Pharaoh who ruled over Egypt. He was very mean to God's people, the Hebrews, and made them work very hard as slaves. He was such an evil ruler that one day he ordered all the Hebrew baby boys to be thrown into the Nile River.

During this time there was a woman who gave birth to a baby boy. She had to hide him from the Egyptians for three months, but eventually she wasn't able to keep him hidden. She put him in a wicker basket and placed him by the bank of the Nile. Miraculously, the daughter of Pharaoh found the basket while she was bathing in the river. When she saw the baby boy, she named him Moses and raised him as her son.

One day, after Moses had become an adult, he saw an Egyptian beating a Hebrew—one of his own people! Out of anger, Moses killed the Egyptian to save the life of the Hebrew slave. When Pharaoh found out about what happened, he ordered Moses to be killed. So Moses ran away to the land of Midian.

One day, after many years living in the land of Midian, God appeared to Moses in the form of a burning bush—yet the fire was not destroying the bush. Moses was amazed! When he turned aside to see this marvelous sight, the voice of God spoke to Him and commanded him to return to Egypt and tell Pharaoh to let the Hebrews go free!

So Moses and his brother Aaron went to Pharaoh and said, "Let my people go!" Pharaoh refused, so God sent plagues upon the land. Each time Pharaoh refused to listen to Moses and Aaron, God sent another plague: 1) God turned the Nile River into blood. 2) God sent frogs upon the land. 3) God sent gnats upon the land. 4) God sent flies upon the land. 5) God made the Egyptians' cattle get sick. 6) God gave the Egyptians and their animals painful boils on their skin. 7) God sent thunder and hail upon the land. 8) God sent locusts upon the land, which ate all the plants. 9) God sent darkness upon the land.

Even after all of these plagues, Pharaoh still refused to let God's people go. So Moses was sad because he knew what was coming. God told Moses that he was going to send one last plague upon the land—the death of the firstborn son in every home. However, God would not touch the houses that had the blood of a lamb on their doorposts. So Moses told the Hebrews to kill the Passover lamb and spread its blood on the doorposts of their houses so that they would be safe.

That night, the death angel came upon the land and killed every firstborn son of every home that didn't have the blood of the lamb on the doorpost. The next morning, after suffering through this terrible plague, Pharaoh finally had enough and ordered that the Hebrew slaves were to go free. All of the Israelites quickly left Egypt to follow the God of Israel to the Promised Land.

After a short while, Pharaoh changed his mind about letting the Hebrews go. So he ordered his army to go after them. The army chased the Hebrews all the way to the bank of the Red Sea. They were trapped. All of a sudden, God told Moses to lift up his staff and stretch out his hand over the sea. When Moses did this, God immediately divided the sea, creating a path for the Hebrews to cross. After they crossed, they saw the Egyptian army continuing to chase them. So God told Moses to stretch out his hand again. Once Moses did what the Lord said, the sea immediately crashed down on the Egyptians, completely covering their chariots and horsemen in the water.

Thus, God saved the people of Israel that day from the Pharaoh! When the people of Israel saw all that the Lord had done, they feared God and believed in Him.

THE END!

The Second Cup of Wine

The Cup of Deliverance

SEDER LEADER:

This cup represents the second "I will" from Exodus 6:6-7. "I will deliver you from slavery."

This cup reminds us that the Lord promises to deliver us from our bondage like He delivered the Israelites from Egypt. As we take this cup, may we remember the death of the Lamb of God who gave up His life to deliver us from death. Please raise your cup and say the blessing with me.

[Everyone recites the blessing of the wine.]

HEBREW:

Baruch atah Adonai Eloheinu melech ha-olam borei p'ri hagafen.

ENGLISH:

Blessed are you, Lord our God, King of the universe, who creates the fruit of the vine.

[Everyone drinks the second cup.]

Blessing the Matzah

SEDER LEADER:

The matzah represents God's provision. As God's people left Egypt in haste, they didn't have time to make provisions for their journey. They had to trust God as they followed His commandments. After they ran out of food, God provided His people with manna to sustain them. Notice that the matzah is both pierced and has stripes. In the same way, Yeshua was pierced in His hands and feet for our transgressions and striped (whipped) for our iniquity.

This matzah is called the bread of affliction (Deuteronomy 16:3). It reminds us of the suffering the Israelites endured in slavery. It also reminds us of the suffering Yeshua endured to give us salvation. This same bread represents freedom as the Israelites left Egypt in haste and thus didn't have time for their bread to rise. This freedom foreshadowed the freedom from our sin that was provided by Yeshua.

READER:

Jesus said to them, "I am the bread of life; whoever comes to me shall not hunger, and whoever believes in me shall never thirst. (John 6:35)

[Seder Leader lifts up piece of matzah.]

SEDER LEADER:

This is the bread of affliction. All who are needy, all who are hungry, come and eat.

[Everyone recites the blessing of the matzah.]

HEBREW:

Baruch atah Adonai Eloheinu melech ha-olam hamotzi lechem min ha-aretz

ENGLISH:

Blessed are you, Lord our God, King of the universe, who brings forth bread from the earth.

[Everyone eats a piece of matzah.]

Tasting the Bitter Herbs

SEDER LEADER:

The bitter herbs represent the bitterness of slavery in Egypt as well as the bitterness that comes as a result of our sin.

[Everyone spreads horseradish onto a piece of matzah.]

SEDER LEADER:

This is symbolic of the bitterness that comes as a result of walking in sin. As we eat the matzah with the horseradish, we are to remember the bitterness of our lives spent in slavery to sin and thank the Father for delivering us through the blood of Yeshua.

[Everyone eats the matzah with horseradish.]

[Everyone spreads charoseth and horseradish together onto a piece of matzah.]

SEDER LEADER:

This is symbolic of when Adam and Eve ate from the tree of the knowledge of good and evil. This is the lifestyle that many of us live today—a mixture of good and evil. The Book of Revelation describes this kind of believer as "lukewarm" (Revelation 3:16). As we eat the matzah with the mixture of charoseth and horseradish, we are to ask God to empower us to walk in purity and holiness so that our lives represent the pure sweetness of the charoseth without any bitter mixture.

[Everyone eats the matzah with the mixture of charoseth and horseradish.]

[Everyone spreads only charoseth onto a piece of matzah.]

SEDER LEADER:

The charoseth represents the pure truth of God's Word and the sweetness that comes as a result of walking in His ways and being filled with His Spirit.

36

READER:

Blessed is the man who walks not in the counsel of the wicked, nor stands in the way of sinners, nor sits in the seat of scoffers; but his delight is in the law of the Lord, and on his law he meditates day and night. He is like a tree planted by streams of water that yields its fruit in its season, and its leaf does not wither. In all that he does, he prospers. (Psalm 1:1-3)

[Everyone eats the matzah with charoseth.]

Eat the Festival Meal

At this time, everyone enjoys a special meal prepared by the host. Traditional foods include things like Matzah Ball Soup, which is a mixture of matzah meal, eggs, water, and chicken fat. Another favorite is Baklava, which is a pastry made with thin layers of unleavened dough, honey, and nuts.

Of course, you can have your own traditions concerning what types of foods to prepare. Obviously the one restriction is that it should be "kosher for Passover," i.e., no leaven.

[Seder Leader prays and gives thanks for the meal.]

Search for the Afikomen

SEDER LEADER:

The afikomen represents the broken body of Yeshua, which was wrapped in linen after His crucifixion and "hidden" in the tomb. The appearance of the matzah recalls the piercing of Yeshua's flesh. In John 6:51, Yeshua explains that the matzah that was broken for us is representative of His body.

READER:

I am the living bread that came down from heaven. If anyone eats of this bread, he will live forever. And the bread that I will give for the life of the world is my flesh. (John 6:51)

READER:

But he was pierced for our transgressions; he was crushed for our iniquities; upon him was he chastisement that brought us peace, and with his wounds we are healed. (Isaiah 53:5)

SEDER LEADER:

The search for the afikomen represents the fact that we must search for the Messiah. The Gospel of Luke says that if we diligently seek Him, we will find Him (Luke 11:10). Are you kids ready to find the akikomen? The one who finds it will receive a reward!

[All the children now search for the afikomen.]

[When the afikomen is found, everyone recites the following blessing]

HEBREW:

Baruch atah Adonai Eloheinu melech ha-olam hamotzi lechem min ha-aretz

ENGLISH:

Blessed are you, Lord our God, King of the universe, who brings forth bread from the earth.

[Everyone breaks of a piece from the afikomen and eats it.]

The Third Cup of Wine

The Cup of Redemption

SEDER LEADER:

This cup represents the third "I will" from Exodus 6:6-7. "I will redeem you with an outstretched arm." The Lord promises to redeem us. We drink this cup to remember our redemption through Yeshua.

READER:

And he took a cup, and when he had given thanks he gave it to them, saying, "Drink of it, all of you, for this is my blood of the covenant, which is poured out for many for the forgiveness of sins." (Matthew 26:27)

[Everyone recites the blessing over the wine.]

HEBREW:

Baruch atah Adonai Eloheinu melech ha-olam borei p'ri hagafen.

ENGLISH:

Blessed are you, Lord our God, King of the universe, who creates the fruit of the vine.

[Everyone drinks the third cup.]

The Cup of Elijah

SEDER LEADER:

This cup is to recall the prophecy that Elijah must return to prepare the way for the Messiah. This cup is filled and then left on the table. Both the Jewish people and Christians are waiting for the return of the Messiah. The Jewish people are waiting for what they believe to be the first coming of Messiah, while Christians are waiting for the Second Coming.

READER:

Behold, I am going to send you Elijah the prophet before the coming of the great and terrible day of the Lord. (Malachi 4:5)

[One of the children opens the door to symbolically welcome in Elijah.]

SEDER LEADER:

Yeshua's return is tied to the Jewish people accepting Him. Yeshua will return to Jerusalem (Zechariah 14). However, He said that Jerusalem will not see Him again until the inhabitants of the city say, "Blessed is he that comes in the name of the Lord" (Matthew 23:37-39). Paul wrote, "For if their [the Jews] rejection means the reconciliation of the world, what will their acceptance mean but life from the dead?" (Romans 11:15). Paul is saying that the salvation of the Jewish people is tied to the resurrection of the just, which occurs at the Second Coming of our Lord!

It is imperative, therefore, that we pray for the salvation of the Jewish people, and everyone else who does not yet know Yeshua as their Savior.

[In his own words, the Seder Leads leads everyone in prayer for the Jewish people and everyone else who does not yet know Yeshua.]

The Fourth Cup of Wine

The Cup of Restoration

SEDER LEADER:

This cup represents the fourth "I will" from Exodus 6:6-7. The Lord promises to make us His people and "acquire us as a nation." In Luke 22:20, Yeshua said that He would not drink the fruit of the vine again until He is with us in His Father's Kingdom. As we drink this fourth cup, we anticipate His promise being fulfilled when we are all together with Him in His Kingdom and everything is finally restored.

READER:

Praise the Lord, all nations! Extol him, all peoples! For great is his steadfast love toward us, and the faithfulness of the Lord endures forever. Praise the Lord! (Psalm 117:1-2)

READER:

The stone that the builders rejected has become the cornerstone. This is the Lord's doing; it is marvelous in our eyes. (Psalm 118:22-23)

[Everyone recites the blessing over the wine.]

HEBREW:

Baruch atah Adonai Eloheinu melech ha-olam borei p'ri hagafen.

ENGLISH:

Blessed are you, Lord our God, King of the universe, who creates the fruit of the vine.

[Everyone drinks the fourth cup.]

Everyone Shouts:

"Next Year in Jerusalem!"

This is shouted in anticipation of the coming of our Lord when we will have the Passover meal with Him in His Kingdom.

We pray that this Passover Haggadah was helpful. May God bring you into a closer and more intimate relationship with Him this Passover season!

About Freedom Hill Community

Freedom Hill is a Messiah-centered community of believers and media-driven ministry based in St. Charles, MO. We are devoted to proclaiming the Gospel of Yeshua (Jesus) and pursuing the roots of our Christian faith. We follow the Scriptures and encourage individuals and families to live for Yeshua with a foundation of the Spirit and the Truth.

In light of our passion to pursue the roots of our Christian faith, one of our goals is to help our Christian brothers and sisters rediscover the beauty and value of the Torah. Why? Because Torah observance is an important part of the life and message of our Messiah. It was prophesied that the Messiah would "elevate the Torah and make it honorable" (Isaiah 42:21). Indeed, Yeshua rested on the Sabbath every seventh day, kept the biblical feast days, and didn't eat unclean animals. The word *Christian* literally means "Follower of Christ." As Christians, we are to walk as Yeshua walked (1 John 2:6). Since Yeshua kept and taught the Torah, it is appropriate for us to do the same.

In addition, the original Christian movement that emerged out of Yeshua's teachings continued to keep the Torah throughout the New Testament. In fact, Yeshua's instructions to His disciples just prior to His ascension were to make disciples of "all the nations" and teach them all that He had commanded them (Matthew 28:19-20). The New Covenant established by Yeshua is intended to write the Torah on our hearts through the work of the Holy Spirit (Jeremiah 31:33). Thus, a return to a Christianity as originally taught and practiced by Messiah and the apostles must include a desire to keep the Sabbath, feasts, and dietary instructions in the Torah.

But where do we begin in reaching our Christian brothers and sisters with these truths? As a ministry, our plan is simply to continue developing resources—everything from simple introductions to the Sabbath and feasts to deeper biblical studies on these important truths and how to defend them. In addition to this book, we have a growing library of articles and sermons available for free on our website. Our teachers and pastors speak about these topics every week at our local congregation as well as at Christian/Messianic conferences and congregations throughout the United States.

If God puts it on your heart to partner with us in carrying out this vision, we could use your support in the following ways. First, we ask that you keep us in prayer. Pray that God will continue to guide and direct our steps. Second, we ask that you consider donating to Freedom Hill Community. You can give online through a one-time donation or set up a recurring monthly donation on our website (www.FreedomHillCommunity.com). Personal checks can be made out to Freedom Hill Community and mailed to the following address:

Freedom Hill Community
P.O. Box 1865
St. Charles, MO 63302-1865

Third, please spread the word about Freedom Hill Community. Sign up to our newsletter on our website so you never miss an update. Share our articles and videos on social media. Consider inviting one of our teachers to come speak at your congregation.

Your support makes it possible for us to share the Gospel of Yeshua and the Torah with people around the world. Thank you for partnering with us in reaching the nations.

Made in the USA
Monee, IL
22 March 2023